201
GREAT
QUESTIONS

Jerry D. Jones

NAVPRESS

A MINISTRY OF THE NAVIGATORS

P.O.BOX 35001, COLORADO SPRINGS, COLORADO 80935

The Navigators is an international Christian organization. Our mission is to reach, disciple, and equip people to know Christ and to make Him known through successive generations. We envision multitudes of diverse people in the United States and every other nation who have a passionate love for Christ, live a lifestyle of sharing Christ's love, and multiply spiritual laborers among those without Christ.

NavPress is the publishing ministry of The Navigators. NavPress publications help believers learn biblical truth and apply what they learn to their lives and ministries. Our mission is to stimulate spiritual formation among our readers.

ISBN 08910-92846

Printed in the United States of America

8 9 10 11 12 13 / 99 98 97

*"A man cannot ask another a question
without at the same time
answering it himself."*

PAUL VALERY

INTRODUCTION

We are living in an era when the art of conversation is almost a thing of the past. The television talks to us more than we talk to one another. Yet at the same time, there is a growing hunger for closeness, for being known and understood. As George Gallup, Jr., states it, "[This generation has] an intensified search for meaningful relationships . . . [for] rediscovering each other."

This little book is an attempt to help each of us do a better job of "connecting" with the people in our lives, to rediscover what it means to really listen to—and learn about—those we most care about.

These questions are intended to be used as:
· Conversation starters.
· A springboard for getting better acquainted with both old and new friends.
· A way to encourage and stimulate the serendipitous rediscovery of one another.
· A way to get to know ourselves better as we discuss our feelings and beliefs with others.
· A way to discuss and, in so doing, better formulate

our ethical, moral, and spiritual beliefs.
· A non-threatening, relaxed way to build bridges with those we don't know well.

Some suggested places to use this book:
· In the living room or around the dinner table.
· While traveling with friends or family. (One handy place to keep this book would be in the glove box of your automobile.)
· During the opening minutes of your small group discussion, Bible study, or Sunday school class to help members get better acquainted.
· On a date.
· At a party.

The questions have been divided into three categories, progressing from lighter questions to those that require a greater degree of group understanding and trust.

Our hope is that *201 Great Questions* will encourage and challenge you to do a better job of "connecting" with the people in your life. It is only in the sharing of who we are with one another that we are best able to love, care, and trust.

In closing, just a reminder that the use of questions to stimulate conversation and thought is no new thing. One of the greatest question askers who ever lived was a man named Jesus. And one of the greatest questions He ever asked was, "Who do you say I am?" (Matthew 16:15). As you launch into this book of questions, responding to His question might be the best place to begin.

May this book begin many warm, invigorating conversations . . .

WARMUP
QUESTIONS

1. If you were to be stranded on an island for the rest of your life, who is the one person in your circle of family or friends that you would most want to be stranded with? Who would you least want to be stranded with? Why?

2. If you could climb into "cartoon land," which cartoon character would you most like to be? Why?

If you were to take a 10-day trip in a car with your family or friends, what would they most likely hear you complain about?

3.

If God put you completely in charge of creating heaven, what would it be like?

4.

5. If you didn't have to worry about making a living, what would you most like to do for the rest of your life?

6. What (or who) most encourages the little child in you to come out and play? When was the last time this happened?

What is your earliest memory? **7.**

As a child, were you ever **8.** spanked? If so, for what reason? Would you use this same form of punishment with your children in similar circumstances? Why or why not?

9. Describe your dream vacation. Who would it be with, where would you go, and what would you do?

10. What is the one thing you never did in high school that you wish you would have done?

If you could live in any other time period, past or future, what period would you choose? Why?

11.

What movie or TV program have you seen in the last year that you wish all your friends could see?

12.

13. What has been one of the most memorable compliments you've received as an adult? Can you remember a special compliment you received as a child?

14. What motivates you most to go to work each day: money or personal satisfaction? If money were not an issue, would you still keep your job?

If someone gave you enough money to start a business of your own, what kind of business would you start?

15.

What is the best imaginable thing that could happen to you during the next five years? How do you think you would handle it?

16.

17. If your life were to become a major motion picture, who would you like to play you? Why? (The person who plays you doesn't have to be a movie star.)

18. If you knew that tomorrow would be the last full day of your life, how would you spend the day?

How would you describe yourself (without mentioning anything about what you do for
a living)?

19.

If you were a mouse, what
would be the most daring thing
you would try to do while the
cat was away?

20.

21. If you were forced to leave North America, where would you go? Why?

22. What is your most important goal in life right now? Will your life change in some way if that goal is reached? If so, how?

Someone has just offered you $50,000 to free-fall to the ground from a helicopter 300 feet in the air. All the details of this fall have been carefully worked out by experts. On the ground will be a huge airbag used by professional stuntmen to break their fall. Providing that you jump right and hit the bag, you will be safe. Will you do this jump? Would you do it for $1,000,000?

24. If the people who know you best were asked, would they say you tend to be mostly predictable or unpredictable? Why? Which of these traits do you most value in a friend? Do you tend to follow a set routine or do you often do the same things differently?

How old were you when you had your first real date? Was it a pleasant experience? Do you know where that person is today?

25.

What social situations tend to make you most flustered and nervous? Why?

26.

27. What is the most fun party you have ever attended? What is the most unusual or different party you have ever attended? What would your ideal party be like?

For $10,000 would you be willing to stand up spontaneously and sing *The Star Spangled Banner* at the top of your lungs in the middle of a church service?

28.

What is usually the first thing that comes to your mind when you think about God?

29.

30.	How much of your clothing has gone unworn for at least one year? What is the one item of clothing that you would be least likely to get rid of? Why?

31.	What is one of the most fun, creative ways you can imagine to surprise your mate or best friend? Have you ever done this or something similar? If so, what?

What are three things you would most like to accomplish in the next year?

32.

If money were no object, what fun thing would you most like to do?

33.

34. If you had no limitations, how would you redecorate a favorite room in your home?

35. If you were to move to a poor primitive country, what three things would you most miss from your current life?

DIGGING
DEEPER

36. What is the biggest lie you've ever told? Why did you tell it? What were the consequences of telling it, if any?

37. What three things do you believe without any doubts?

Theologian and author A.W. Tozer once said, "A bit of healthy disbelief is sometimes as needful as faith to the welfare of our souls." Do you agree or disagree? Why? Where are you most likely to have some "healthy disbelief"?

39. What is one of the books (other than the Bible) that has had the greatest influence on your life? Why?

40. If God would grant you any one request, what would it be?

If you had the power to re-create yourself, what are the things you would *not* change about yourself?

41.

Is it ever OK to waste time? What does this statement mean to you: "Activity that does not result in progress toward a goal is a waste of time"? Do you agree?

42.

43. Concerning you and me, have your expectations of our relationship been surpassed or disappointed? In what ways?

44. One day God is sitting around visiting with the angels and He begins to speak highly of you. In His proud, fatherly way, what would He say that would show He was pleased with you?

Under what circumstances do you feel most lonely? Least lonely? Why?

45.

What do you need to change or improve in your life right now to help you have better relationships? What frustrates you most about your current relationships? What pleases you most?

46.

47. Survivors of a plane crash often credit their survival to prayer. How much do you think prayer is the determining factor between those who survive and those who do not?

48. What do you look forward to most about growing old? Least?

Which one of the following traits do you think is the most important to instill in a child's life?

49.

    obedience
    conformity
    tolerance of
      opposing views
    patriotism
    good manners
    independence (thinking
      and acting for yourself)

Why? Which of these traits do you think is least important to instill in children? Why?

50. Describe a time when you felt frightened. What were the circumstances? What helps soothe you most during times of fear?

51. If you could relive any part of your life, what part would it be and why?

Have either of your parents
ever told you they were sorry—
or asked for your forgiveness—
for something they did? If yes,
what were the circumstances
and how did it make you feel
about them afterwards?

52.

53. Which *two* of the following qualities do you think are most important to have in a marriage partner?
undying loyalty
sense of humor
intellectual stimulation
compatible religious
    preferences
attractiveness
popularity
relaxed temperament
communication skills
Which of these two do you value least? Why?

What is the most difficult choice you've had to make in your life up to this point? Why was it difficult? What factors helped you make that choice?

54.

Do you believe that God has only one perfect mate for everyone?

55.

56. At this time in your life are you experiencing mostly contentment or discontent in the following areas?

in your job
in your relationships
in your spiritual life
in your home life

Why?

Would you marry someone of another skin color (race)? Why or why not? How would your family feel about this if you were to do so?

57.

A close friend of yours is over-eating and gaining weight. Should this be any of your business? Why or why not? What would you say or do, if anything?

58.

59. A football coach once said, "We learn almost nothing in victory, but we learn much in defeat." Do you agree with this? In your own life, have you learned more from your failures or from your successes? Explain.

Is it as easy for you to talk about your failures and goof-ups as it is to talk about your successes? Why?

60.

What would be the most difficult thing to forgive someone for? What if it were something done to you personally? If done to a member of your family?

61.

62. What would you most like people to remember you for after you die?

63. When someone on the street stops you to ask for food money, what do you usually do or say? Why?

If laughter were the fuel in the tank of life, would your gauge show your tank to be full, half-full, or nearly empty? Why? When was the last time you laughed till you cried?

64.

65. What is the most dangerous thing you would like to try doing? What keeps you from doing it?

66. What do you think God's opinion is of you? If you could read His mind, what do you think He would be thinking about you right now?

If you had the power to read people's minds, how would you use it? Whose mind would you most like to read right now?

67.

In your life right now do you feel like you are holding on to things tightly or loosely? Which things are you holding on to more tightly than others? Why?

68.

69. Is there at least one person who knows everything about you? In your opinion, what are the primary advantages and disadvantages in having such a relationship?

What are the biggest questions you have about your relationship with God?

70.

What are the five things you are most thankful for in your life right now? What are some of the things you do to show this thankfulness?

71.

72. In difficult times, who would you most like to have praying for you? Why?

73. What are the things that most inhibit or hurt your relationship with God at this time in your life?

Would you say that the focus of your life right now is more on the development of relationships or on the accomplishment of goals and objectives? What would you like to change about this focus, if anything?

74.

75. What person in your life has been the best example of love? Explain how.

76. What have been the most surprising gifts you've ever received? What were some of the most enjoyable gifts you've ever given to someone else?

What are some of the qualities of your grandparents that you would most like your own children to have? What are some of the qualities of your parents that you'd most like to see passed on to your children?

78. The year is 2010. You have just been informed that planet earth will be destroyed tomorrow. A friend of yours works for NASA and has been able to secure for you three priceless passes on a space shuttle to another planet where you will be safe. Will you personally use one of these passes, knowing that you will be leaving earth, never to return? If this happened today, who would you give the extra passes to? Why would you choose these people?

79.

What were your very first impressions of your spouse or your best friend?

80.

Mother Teresa called you today and said she is very short-staffed and desperately needs your help in India for two years. There is no pay but she can provide a bed for you and simple meals with her staff. She explained that your primary responsibilities would be emptying bedpans and giving spoonfuls of water to the dying. What would you tell her? Why?

81. Because of a computer error, the phone company inadvertently sends you a refund check for $1,000. The check is clearly in your name so you are not breaking the law by depositing the check. But you know it is a mistake. Will you deposit the phone company check, hoping they will not catch their mistake (or hoping they will just forgive it if they do), or do you contact the phone company and ask them what they would like you to do with the check? Why? Would your answer change if the check were for only $5.00?

What part of your life right now do you think is "on hold"? What has to happen before you can move on? Is this "on hold" time best described by fear, uncertainty, or excitement? Why?

82.

The Chinese philosopher Mencius once said, "Before a man can do things there must be things he will not do." What are three things you will not do? Why?

83.

84. During WWII German theologian Dietrich Bonhoeffer participated in a conspiracy to assassinate Hitler. Although the conspiracy failed and he was executed for making the effort, do you think Bonhoeffer was right in his attempts to kill Hitler? If you had been Bonhoeffer, would you have participated in this murder conspiracy? Why or why not?

What was the greatest peer
pressure you felt as a teen?
What is the greatest peer
pressure you feel as an adult?
How are you handling it?

85.

What does ugly mean to you?
Describe it.

86.

87. What are three steps you need to take to become the person you were meant to be?

88. What do you consider to be your greatest creative ability or gift? Do you think others fully recognize your creative abilities?

As a child, when you got caught doing something wrong, which of the following were you most likely to do?

> blame someone else
> deny that you did it
> run and hide
> take full responsibility and
>   accept the consequences

What are you most likely to do now as an adult?

90. Do you think you could be incredibly rich and still have a good conscience? Why or why not? How much is too much?

91. How would you counsel a homosexual friend who wants to be a Christian?

What is your definition of love? **92.**
How would you describe the
meaning of love to a child?

Do you think that, in God's **93.**
eyes, some vocations are more
important than others? Why
or why not?

94. When you make choices about right or wrong, what do you consider most: present consequences or future consequences? Why?

A friend of yours works at an auto parts store. Over the past few weeks he has been stealing small items to be used for some repairs on his car. You know that the parts have been stolen. One day, he asks you if you will come help him repair his car. You would be using the stolen parts. What do you do? Do you act as if nothing wrong has happened or do you say something to him about the stolen parts? Why?

96. What are three barriers that keep you from reaching your full potential? What would most help you overcome these barriers?

97. Do you give most of your gifts in order to give love or to receive love? Why? Have you ever purchased a gift for someone to ease your conscience?

Do you think people would be surprised about your thought-life? How often would you be embarrassed if others knew exactly what was on your mind? Do you think your thought-life is better or worse than most of the people in your circle of friends? Why?

99. Someone once said that everything we do is motivated by either love or fear. If that is true, what is it that motivates you most of the time? Why?

One of the women in your neighborhood comes running to your home seeking protection from a violent, abusive husband. Before you have a chance to call the police, her husband shows up at your front door, looking very angry and out of control, asking if his wife is there. How will you handle this situation?

100.

101. The Bible calls us to both love our enemies and to lend, expecting nothing back. Which of these two do you have the hardest time doing? Why?

102. Is there something you would be tempted to do if you knew you would never be found out? Is it primarily evil or good?

103. You are getting ready to hire someone in your office. You have only one open position but you have two *equally qualified* candidates. One is a woman and one is a man. Which one will you most likely hire? Why?

104. Would you be comfortable in a marriage where the wife is the primary wage earner and the husband stays home? Why or why not? What do you most like or dislike about this marriage model?

What is the worst thing that could happen to you if you take a risk and fail? What is the best thing that could happen to you if you take a risk and succeed?

106. How many hugs do you need each day? Are you generally behind or ahead on your need quotient? When is it hardest for you to give or receive hugs from others?

107. Which of your parents has had the greatest influence on your life? How?

Values clarification expert Sid Simon has suggested that everyone should develop his or her own "anti-suicide list"—at least fifty reasons why you should not kill yourself. If you were to develop such a list for yourself, what are at least five things you would put on that list?

109. Does God like to have fun? If so, how would you describe the fun-loving side of God? If not, why not?

110. What would you consider to be your greatest hunger besides food? Is it a healthy or unhealthy hunger?

There is an old saying, "If you crawl from one nest to another, you will never learn to fly." What are the nests in your life that have a tendency to keep you from flying?

111.

112. What has been the hardest letter you've ever written or the hardest phone call you've ever had to make?

What is the worst way you can imagine dying? The best way? Do you think you will die before your time?

113.

114. A friend of yours is making wedding plans to marry someone she just met one month ago. She is seriously talking about getting married in three weeks. Would you encourage her to slow down the wedding plans? Why or why not? Would you respond any differently if "she" was a "he"?

What do you usually do when you feel like there is distance growing between you and a good friend? **115.**

What is the worst rejection you've ever experienced? How did you handle it? **116.**

117. What do you wish others knew or understood about you that you think they usually don't?

In what area do you need more self-confidence at this stage in your life? What specific compliments or affirmations would you like to be hearing more often?

118.

119. Is there a particular fear in your life that you have overcome? If so, how did you overcome it? What is the one fear you most wish you could overcome now?

What is one of your best childhood memories? What is one of the worst?

120.

121. What object or possession in your home or apartment has the greatest amount of meaning to you personally? Why?

Which one of your accomplishments over the past year or two do you feel best about? Why?

122.

123. If tomorrow you were given a choice—all expenses paid— between spending a month helping feed and care for the starving in Ethiopia or a month relaxing on an island in the South Pacific, which would you choose? Why?

How would you describe God to a child? **124.**

Do you think it is possible to live with no regrets? Explain. **125.**

126. When you are visiting with a close friend, do you generally find yourself more interested in talking about yourself, or listening and learning about your friend? Is this also true when you are visiting with a stranger?

Whose marriage do you most consider to be a model marriage? What is it about their marriage that you most admire?

127.

128. What is your definition of success? Do you consider yourself successful? How would your definition of success be different from that of an Ethiopian mother with a child on the verge of starvation?

What is the one thing in life that you care most deeply about? Does everyone in your circle of friends and family know this about you?

129.

130. If you were to die tomorrow, what would you want people to remember as your most important accomplishment?

How much money would you need to make each year to feel rich? What would be the biggest change in your lifestyle? What, if anything, appeals to you about being rich?

131.

132. If you were to change your career/job every seven years, what are some of the different careers you would most like to have during your lifetime?

Of the following things, which would be easiest for you to become addicted to?

money
success
power
sex
alcohol
drugs
work
TV

What other things are potential addictions for you?

134. If you were to pick one place to live for the rest of your life, where would it be? If you were to live several places, where would those places be? Why?

How much is your personal identity and self-worth determined by the job you have and your success at it?

135.

136. Do you tend to choose your friends more because of what they can give you or because of what you can give them? What can you do to be a better friend?

When you choose your clothing, what image are you hoping to project? When buying clothes, do you think you generally spend too much, too little, or just the right amount?

137.

138. When you see something in a store that you want but can't afford, how do you feel? What do you do?

George Gallup, Jr., reports that approximately one-half of born-again evangelicals do not attend church on a regular basis. Do you think it is important for a Christian to attend church? What are the most important things you look for in a church? If you are presently attending church, what would you change about your church if you could?

140. Have you ever gone back on an agreement with someone? If so, why? Has anyone ever done this to you?

141. Regardless of whether you are single or married, what would you say is the one thing you are most "married" to at this stage in life?

How often do you balance your checkbook? If someone were to look at all the checks you've written over the past year, what would they consider to be your life priorities?

142.

143. If you were to completely stop watching TV for a year, what would you most likely do with the extra time? What would you miss most on TV?

The doctor has informed you that your father is dying of a rare blood disease. It will be a painless death, and will probably happen within six months. In fact, your father will most likely die in his sleep. He is unaware that he has this disease. The doctor has told you that it is up to you whether to tell your father or not. Will you tell him, or will you let him live out his last days as though nothing were wrong? If you were in your father's shoes, would you want someone to let you know? Why?

145. Are you the same person with your family as with your friends? If not, what are the differences? Why?

Do you believe that God specifically designates how long each person will live, or do you think He allows circumstances to determine that?

146.

147. What is the most embarrassing thing that has ever happened to you? What is the most embarrassing thing you can imagine happening to you?

How much of an influence do **148.** you think you have on your family? Your friends? Your co-workers? Your boss? In your church? Do you wish you had more influence than you do? What changes do you think you would need to make to have greater influence?

149. You have been given the responsibility to distribute 20 million dollars to help the world be a better place. Where you give this money is totally up to you. How would you distribute it?

What living person is closest to being your hero? A person who is no longer living? Why these particular persons?

150.

151. Someone once said that "God has given us all the time we need to do the things He wants us to do." Do you agree with this statement? Do you think the main reason we seem to have so little time is because we are doing things God doesn't want us to do? Why or why not?

What is the most beautiful thing you have ever seen? Heard? What is the most beautiful thing you have in your home? Why?

153.

How much effect does someone's physical appearance have on your first impressions of him or her? How often do your first impressions change once you have a chance to get to know a person? How reliable are your first impressions?

What are the three questions
you would most like to ask God? **154.**

If you were given an oppor-
tunity to have any one part of
your body remade exactly the
way you wanted it, what would
you change? Would you still
make this change even if you
knew it would take off five years
of your life? Ten? **155.**

156. What is the worst thing possible you can ever imagine happening to you? How do you think you would deal with it? What kind of support would you need? Do you think you have that kind of support in your life right now?

157. When are you most happy? Are other people necessary for your happiness? Why or why not?

As a child, how was affection expressed in your family? How would it have been different if it had been totally up to you?

158.

How well do you handle compliments? Is it easier for you to give them or receive them? Why?

159.

160. You ask a relatively new friend of the opposite sex to go with you to a movie. The sex and nudity is much more graphic than you had anticipated and you're feeling uncomfortable watching it. You are unsure how your friend feels. What will you do?

Describe a time when you stole something and got caught. Describe a time when you stole something and did not get caught. When was the last time you had a temptation to steal something, even something very small? Is there any case in which stealing would be legitimate?

162. What is the worst job you can imagine? Would you be willing to do this job for the rest of your life if it paid $300,000 a year? Would you be willing to do this job if it meant that there would be less suffering and hunger in the world? Do you think that God ever calls us to do jobs that we hate for the betterment of mankind?

When was the last time you
asked someone to forgive you?
How did he or she respond?

163.

What do you consider to be your
five greatest strengths? Your
five greatest weaknesses?

164.

165. Which is more important to you: work and accomplishments or people and family? How does your weekly schedule reflect this?

How can people tell if you are angry? Is it usually easy or hard to tell?

166.

167.

When making decisions, do you put more trust in facts or in feelings? Are you pleased with most of your decisions?

What kind of people bring out the best in you? What two or three people in particular? Why?

168.

169. When was the last time you said "I'm sorry" to another person? How difficult is it for you to use the words "I'm sorry"?

In what areas of your life is it
most difficult to trust God?
Other people? Yourself?

170.

171. If you were a single mom or dad, what do you think would be the most difficult things you'd have to face?

172. What are the three most important things in your daily schedule?

What does contentment mean to you? How close to contentment are you in your life right now? What would need to change for you to experience greater contentment?

174. Does God ever make us do things, or does He always leave the choice up to us?

What would be the advantages and disadvantages of having arranged marriages? Do you think it would produce better or worse marriages? Why?

175.

PROBE
QUESTIONS

176. You are about to get married. How much of your past should you discuss together? Which areas of your past experience do you think are most important to talk about?

What are the circumstances in which you feel most susceptible to temptation at this stage in your life? What are you doing to minimize these temptations?

177.

178. When was the last time you told someone in person that you loved him or her? When was the last time someone told you face-to-face that he or she loved you? How do you express your love?

Is there someone in your life that you can't stand or can barely tolerate? What bothers you most about this person?

180. What do you consider to be one of your greatest personal failures to date? What was the most important lesson you gained from this failure?

Do you consider suicide to be murder? How do you think God views suicide? **181.**

182. Would you say that you live your life primarily by legalism or by grace? What is the difference between the two? What are the signs that tell if a person is living by one or the other?

Do you sometimes say and do things to make yourself appear more important in the eyes of others? Do you ever exaggerate or lie in an attempt to make yourself look good? If yes, when are you most tempted to do this?

183.

184. Your mother has a debilitating case of Parkinson's disease. The doctor has informed you that the only chance for a cure is to use a new medication developed from aborted fetuses. The alternative for your mother is a long, agonizing deterioration. The choice is yours. Will you opt for the new medication or will you decline it? Why?

If you should ever be in a fatal car accident, would you want any of your body parts donated to help someone else live or have a better quality of life? Why or why not?

186. What do you wish you would never have to worry about again? Why?

187. What would cause you to distrust your mate the most? What could your mate do to rebuild that trust again? Has someone ever mistrusted you unfairly? Why?

Is there any person or cause you'd be willing to *die* for? What cause are you *living* for now? Explain.

188.

189. Is there anything that you think is too personal to be discussed with your mate? With your best friend? With your parents? With your pastor or a counselor? Which of these people would it be easiest for you to tell your deepest, darkest secrets?

Is there at least one person in your life that you know beyond the shadow of a doubt loves you just the way you are? What are some of your traits that may be hindering others from loving and accepting you the way you would like to be loved and accepted?

190.

191. After your death, would you prefer to be buried or cremated? Why?

192. When are you most likely to use laughter to cover up your true feelings? What masks other than laughter do you most often use?

Has there been a time in the past year or two when God seemed especially real or close to you? If so, explain.

193.

194. Have you ever received professional counseling? Was it helpful? Why do you think today's generation seems to have a much greater need to seek counseling than did our parents' or grandparents' generation?

Define deep personal faith.
How would you describe your
own experience of faith?

195.

196. Does a married woman have the right to allow herself to get pregnant because she wants to have a child, even though her husband has clearly stated that he does not want a child?

197. C.S. Lewis said, "God whispers in our pleasures but shouts in our pain." How is God whispering and shouting to you in your life?

198. What is the one memory or image in your mind that you most wish you could forget?

Do you believe there is a hell?
How would you describe it?
What would you do to keep
from ending up there?

199.

200. Under what circumstances would you be willing to kill another person?

Where are you in your spiritual journey right now? Where would you like to be?

201.

Author

Jerry D. Jones is the editor of *Single Adult Ministries Journal* (*SAM Journal*), based in Colorado Springs, Colorado. Jerry is also director of the Singles Ministry Resources (a division of the David C. Cook Foundation).